The Global Game - The Evolution Of Football

While every precaution has been taken in the preparation of this book, the publisher assumes no responsibility for errors or omissions, or for damages resulting from the use of the information contained herein.

THE GLOBAL GAME - THE EVOLUTION OF FOOTBALL

First edition. October 4, 2023.

Copyright © 2023 PA BOOKS.

ISBN: 979-8215069202

Written by PA BOOKS.

Table of Contents

Chapter 1: The Ancient Roots - Football in Antiquity

———

In the grand tapestry of human history, few pursuits have captured the imagination and united communities quite like the sport of football. As we embark on this journey through time, let us harken back to the very dawn of civilization, where the roots of this beloved game find their earliest traces.

The Sumerians, who inhabited the fertile lands of Mesopotamia around 2500 BCE, are often heralded as the forebearers of football. In the midst of their great cities and complex societies, they devised a game that involved a spherical object being kicked about a field. While this primitive rendition of football may bear little resemblance to the contemporary sport, it laid the essential groundwork upon which football's evolution would unfold.

It is crucial to recognize that the concept of football, or some form of it, was not exclusive to Mesopotamia. Across the ancient world, in diverse civilizations and cultures, the idea of a game involving a ball and feet found resonance. It was as if the very essence of football was inscribed in the human spirit, waiting to manifest itself in various forms.

Venturing to ancient Greece, we uncover yet another tantalizing chapter in the prehistory of football. There, a game known as "episkyros" or "harpaston" thrived during the 4th and 3rd centuries BCE. This early incarnation of the sport featured two teams locked in spirited competition, with the aim of propelling a ball over the opposing team's goal line. While rudimentary by modern standards, this ancient game shared the fundamental objective of scoring goals, foreshadowing the essence of what football would come to embody.

Traverse further eastward, and we encounter the ancient Chinese sport of "cuju," which flourished during the Han Dynasty (206 BCE – 220 CE). In cuju, players demonstrated remarkable skill and precision as they used their feet to guide a leather ball through a small opening. This distant ancestor of modern football bore testament to the universality of the human inclination toward kicking a ball with vigor and artistry.

Chapter 2: Medieval Origins - Early Ball Games and Mob Football

During the tumultuous medieval era, football's earliest roots began to intertwine with the fabric of society. This was an age marked by feudalism, chivalry, and a thirst for entertainment that gave rise to a raucous and unruly precursor to the modern game. In this chapter, we step into the medieval world, where the origins of football were far from the pristine pitches and organized leagues of today but were instead forged in the crucible of early ball games and the chaos of mob football.

Medieval England: Birthplace of the Mob Football Spectacle

Picture yourself in medieval England, a land of castles, knights, and serfs, where life was rugged and often rife with conflict. In the midst of this tumultuous period, the stage was set for the emergence of a sport that would capture the imagination of the masses - mob football.

Mob football, a term aptly named for the sheer tumult it engendered, was a game played in towns and villages across England. It had few rules, if any, and even fewer boundaries. The objectives were straightforward: get the ball to a predetermined location or, at times, into the opposing team's church.

The true spectacle of mob football lay in its chaos. Entire communities would participate, and the boundaries between sport and combat blurred as passionate players and spectators alike threw themselves into the fray. It was a raw and unbridled expression of communal spirit, reflecting the fierce and untamed nature of the times.

Early Attempts at Regulation and Order

Despite the mayhem, or perhaps because of it, mob football held a special place in the hearts of medieval communities. However, it wasn't long before attempts were made to impose some semblance of order on this unruly game. Early attempts at regulation emerged as various regions developed their own localized versions of football.

These localized variants introduced rudimentary rules, such as restrictions on handling the ball with the hands and designated goal locations. In some regions, the game was played on Shrove Tuesday or other festival days, further cementing its place in the social calendar.

Yet, it's essential to note that these rules varied widely from place to place. The chaotic spirit of mob football endured, with each locality infusing its unique flavor into the game. In some areas, there were no limits to the number of players on each team, while in others, restrictions were imposed to bring a modicum of order.

Mob Football: A Cultural Touchstone

Medieval mob football was more than just a sport; it was a cultural touchstone. It transcended the boundaries of class and status, uniting people in a shared passion. In the frenzy of the game, the rigid hierarchies of medieval society dissolved, and individuals from all walks of life came together as equals on the field.

As we delve deeper into the annals of history, it becomes evident that mob football was more than just a precursor to modern football; it was a reflection of the times. It spoke to the spirit of a society in flux, where tradition clashed with innovation, and where the thrill of the game held the power to unite and ignite the passions of an entire community.

Chapter 3: Birth of the Modern Game - The Codification of Football

As we transition from the raucous and unruly days of medieval football, we step into an era marked by a thirst for order and structure. It is here that the story of the modern game truly begins - an era defined by the codification of football, where rules were established, and the foundations of organized play were laid.

A Patchwork of Regional Variations

In the wake of medieval mob football, the need for standardized rules became increasingly evident. Each region had developed its own unique variant of the game, and as a result, football was a patchwork of regional variations. To play a game in one town might be an entirely different experience than in a neighboring village. This lack of uniformity posed challenges, especially for inter-community matches.

The Cambridge Rules: A Milestone in Football History

Enter the Cambridge Rules, a pioneering set of regulations that would play a pivotal role in the development of modern football. These rules, drawn up by students at Cambridge University in 1848, sought to standardize the game and establish a common framework for play. They introduced critical elements that remain fundamental to football today, such as the prohibition of using hands to touch the ball, the concept of fouls, and the introduction of referees.

The Cambridge Rules marked a significant departure from the free-for-all chaos of medieval football. They brought a degree of order and structure to the game, providing players with a clear set of guidelines to follow. This newfound clarity paved the way for more refined tactics, strategy, and skill development.

The Sheffield Rules: An Alternative Path

While the Cambridge Rules were gaining traction in the south of England, the town of Sheffield in the north took a slightly different path. In 1858, Sheffield Football Club codified their own set of rules, known as the Sheffield Rules. These rules differed in some respects from the Cambridge Rules, most notably in their allowance of handling the ball, albeit with some restrictions.

The existence of multiple sets of rules was a testament to the ongoing experimentation and evolution of the game. Different regions clung to their preferred variations, resulting in a fascinating tapestry of football traditions.

The Birth of Football Associations

The desire for standardization and uniformity eventually led to the formation of football associations. In 1863, representatives from various clubs met at the Freemasons' Tavern in London to establish the Football Association (FA). This historic gathering resulted in the official adoption of the Cambridge Rules as the foundation for the modern game. The FA also introduced the concept of the football field's dimensions, an area of play we now take for granted.

The establishment of the FA laid the groundwork for organized competition and a shared framework for football. Other associations soon followed suit, with Scotland forming its own association in 1873 and Wales and Ireland following shortly thereafter.

The Proliferation of Clubs and Competition

With standardized rules in place, the number of football clubs began to proliferate. Clubs that had previously played under their own localized rules now had a common code to adhere to. This burgeoning club scene paved the way for organized competitions, and the FA Cup was born in 1871, becoming the world's oldest football competition. The competitive spirit of football was on full display, captivating the imaginations of players and fans alike.

The Birth of International Play

The codification of football rules also set the stage for international competition. The first international match took place in 1872 when England faced off against Scotland, showcasing the power of football to transcend borders and unite nations.

Chapter 4: The Early Clubs - Formation of Football Clubs

In football's evolution, the codification of rules in the mid-19th century marked a turning point. As the game shed its chaotic past, it embraced structure and order. With clear rules in place, the stage was set for the birth of football clubs, institutions that would go on to shape the sport's identity and community spirit. This chapter delves into the fascinating journey of the early clubs and their pivotal role in the development of football.

The Birth of Club Football

With standardized rules in hand, football enthusiasts sought not only to play the game but also to form dedicated clubs. These clubs were more than just teams; they were communities bound together by a shared passion for the sport. The late 19th century saw the proliferation of football clubs across England, Scotland, and beyond.

Sheffield Football Club - Pioneers of the Game

One of the earliest football clubs to emerge in this era was Sheffield Football Club, founded in 1857. Often referred to as the "world's oldest football club," Sheffield FC played a crucial role in shaping the early development of the sport. Their commitment to the Sheffield Rules, a unique set of football regulations that allowed for handling of the ball to some extent, distinguished them from other clubs adhering to the FA's rules.

Sheffield FC not only played matches but also actively promoted the game's growth. They published the world's first footballing newspaper,

"The Sheffielder," and engaged in matches against other emerging clubs. Their dedication to the sport's development left an indelible mark on football history.

The Corinthian Spirit - Corinthian Football Club

While some clubs focused primarily on competition, others embraced the Corinthian spirit. The Corinthian Football Club, founded in 1882, embodied this ethos. They were known for their sportsmanship, fair play, and gentlemanly conduct on and off the field. The Corinthians demonstrated that football was not just about winning but also about embodying the spirit of the game.

The club embarked on international tours, playing against teams from various countries. Their approach to the sport transcended national boundaries and served as a model for how football could foster goodwill and camaraderie across the world.

The Formation of Leagues

As more clubs sprang up, the need for structured competition became apparent. The 1880s witnessed the birth of football leagues, beginning with the establishment of the Football League in England in 1888. This groundbreaking development introduced the concept of a regular schedule of matches, where clubs competed for the coveted league title. The inaugural season featured 12 teams, including Preston North End, who went on to become the first-ever champions.

Football's Community Impact

Football clubs quickly became central to their communities. They provided a sense of identity and belonging, fostering local pride and camaraderie. Supporters flocked to matches, and stadiums became the epicenters of excitement and passion. The bonds forged among fans and players alike created a unique football culture that endures to this day.

Emergence of Rivalries

With the formation of leagues and regular competitions, rivalries began to take shape. These clashes between clubs became the stuff of legends, stirring intense emotions and rivalries that continue to captivate fans worldwide. From the North West derbies of England to the Old Firm rivalry in Scotland, these contests added drama and narrative to the football landscape.

Chapter 5: Evolution of the Rules - From Chaos to Organization

As we continue our journey through the rich history of football, we find ourselves at a pivotal juncture. With the birth of football clubs and the establishment of leagues, the need for precise and universally accepted rules became increasingly apparent. In this chapter, we explore the evolution of football's rules, tracing the path from the chaos of early mob football to the organized structure that underpins the modern game.

The Rulebook Takes Shape

The 19th century saw a multitude of different rulesets employed by various clubs and regions, leading to inconsistencies and disputes on the field. The quest for a standardized rulebook gained momentum, and football associations played a crucial role in this endeavor.

The Football Association's Influence

The Football Association (FA), established in 1863, played a central role in unifying the rules of the game. The adoption of the Cambridge Rules as a basis for the modern game was a significant step forward. The Cambridge Rules introduced several fundamental concepts, including the use of feet, rather than hands, to play the ball and the idea of fouls.

However, the path to standardization was not without its challenges. Some clubs, such as Sheffield FC, continued to adhere to their own rules, leading to occasional clashes between those who followed the FA's guidelines and those who held fast to regional variations.

The Emergence of Referees and Offside Rules

One of the crucial developments in the evolution of the game was the introduction of referees. The role of the referee was to enforce the rules and maintain order on the field. This addition helped curb excessive violence and provided a more structured environment for players.

The offside rule also underwent refinement during this period. Initially, the rule stipulated that a player was offside if they were positioned nearer to the opponent's goal than the ball at the moment it was played to them. This led to numerous disputes and debates. In 1866, a significant alteration was made to the offside rule, requiring a player to have three opponents between them and the goal line to be considered onside. This change provided more clarity and contributed to the flow of the game.

Standardization Spreads Across Borders

The influence of the FA and standardized rules extended beyond England. Scotland established its own football association in 1873, adopting a ruleset closely aligned with the FA's regulations. The spread of standardized rules paved the way for international competition and the eventual formation of the British Home Championship, a competition featuring teams from the various nations of the United Kingdom.

Challenges and Controversies

Standardization brought about greater consistency, but it also gave rise to new challenges and controversies. Disputes over rule interpretations and contentious decisions by referees became part and parcel of the sport. The debate over the handling of the ball and the nature of fouls continued to evolve, with various interpretations and amendments.

Chapter 6: Pioneers of the Game - Legendary Players and Innovators

As we venture further into the history of football, it becomes clear that the sport's evolution has been driven not only by changes in rules and organizations but also by the remarkable individuals who graced the pitch. This chapter pays tribute to the pioneers of the game, the legendary players, and innovators who left an indelible mark on football's history.

Charles W. Alcock - A Visionary Administrator

Charles W. Alcock, a name that resonates through football's history, was not only a talented player but also a visionary administrator. He is best known for his role in founding the Football Association (FA) and for serving as its secretary for over twenty years. Under his leadership, the FA became the central authority for football in England, overseeing the development and spread of the sport.

Alcock was a pioneer in organizing inter-club competitions and international matches, fostering the growth of football. He was instrumental in the organization of the first FA Cup competition in 1871, an event that would go on to become one of the world's oldest and most prestigious football tournaments.

Dr. James Naismith - The Father of Basketball with Football Roots

While Dr. James Naismith is primarily known for inventing basketball, his background in football played a significant role in shaping the new sport. Born in Canada, Naismith was a talented footballer before moving to the United States. His experience with football influenced the creation of basketball, as he sought to design a game that could be played indoors during the winter months.

The concept of "dribbling" in basketball, where players move the ball while running, bears similarities to football's dribbling technique. Naismith's innovations in sport were not limited to basketball; they were deeply rooted in his love for football and his desire to adapt sports to changing circumstances.

The Emergence of Legendary Players

The late 19th century and early 20th century witnessed the emergence of legendary football players who captivated audiences with their skill and artistry. Players like Dixie Dean, Jimmy Greaves, and Stanley Matthews became household names, celebrated for their goal-scoring prowess, dribbling abilities, and technical finesse.

One of the most iconic figures of this era was Pelé, the Brazilian sensation who dazzled the world with his extraordinary talent. Pelé's remarkable career included three FIFA World Cup victories and countless records broken. His impact extended beyond the pitch, solidifying football's status as a global phenomenon.

Innovations in Playing Styles

The pioneers of the game also played a significant role in shaping football's playing styles. From the tactical brilliance of the Hungarian national team in the 1950s, known as the "Magical Magyars," to the "Total Football" philosophy of the Dutch national team in the 1970s, football witnessed continuous innovation in tactics and strategies.

Chapter 7: Crossing Borders - Football in Europe and Beyond

Football's journey from a localized pastime to a global spectacle was a transformation fueled by the sport's ability to transcend borders and cultures. In this chapter, we explore the expansion of football across Europe and its emergence as a global phenomenon, with the sport's influence reaching far beyond its European heartland.

Football's European Odyssey

As football gained popularity in England, it didn't take long for the sport to cross the English Channel and make its mark on the European continent. The late 19th century witnessed the spread of football clubs in France, Belgium, and the Netherlands. These clubs often had strong ties to British expatriates, who played a pivotal role in introducing and popularizing the game.

In 1904, the Fédération Internationale de Football Association (FIFA) was founded in Paris, marking a crucial step in the internationalization of the sport. FIFA's mission was to oversee and promote football worldwide, fostering cooperation and competition among national associations.

Football's Migration to South America

While Europe was embracing the sport, football was making its way across the Atlantic to South America. British sailors, immigrants, and workers introduced the game to countries like Argentina, Brazil, and Uruguay. These nations quickly fell in love with football, developing their unique styles and traditions.

The South American passion for football was undeniable, and it was on display when Uruguay hosted the inaugural FIFA World Cup in 1930, winning the tournament in front of an adoring home crowd. The success of South American teams on the world stage cemented the continent's status as a football powerhouse.

The Global Reach of the World Cup

The FIFA World Cup, inaugurated in 1930, stands as one of the most significant milestones in football's global journey. The tournament brought together nations from around the world, showcasing the sport's universal appeal. The World Cup became a stage for national pride, cultural exchange, and international cooperation.

Over the decades, the World Cup has captured the hearts of billions, with iconic moments and legendary players etching their names into football history. The tournament's ability to unite nations and transcend political and cultural differences has made it the most-watched sporting event globally.

Football's Expansion to New Frontiers

As the 20th century unfolded, football continued to expand its reach, reaching new frontiers. Africa embraced the sport, producing legendary players like George Weah and Samuel Eto'o, and hosting the World Cup in 2010, bringing the tournament to the African continent for the first time.

Asia, too, became a hub for football development, with nations like Japan and South Korea making their mark on the international stage. The AFC Asian Cup and the rise of football leagues in the Middle East, such as the Qatar Stars League, reflected the sport's growth in the region.

Chapter 8: The World Cup Saga - Globalization of Football

The FIFA World Cup, often referred to as the "greatest show on Earth," has been at the forefront of football's globalization. In this chapter, we embark on a journey through the World Cup saga, tracing the tournament's evolution from its humble beginnings to its status as a global phenomenon that unites nations and transcends borders.

Birth of a Dream - Uruguay 1930

The inaugural FIFA World Cup in 1930 was a momentous occasion in the history of football. Hosted by Uruguay, the tournament featured 13 teams, including European powerhouses like Argentina, Chile, and Yugoslavia, who made the long journey across the Atlantic. Uruguay emerged victorious, winning the hearts of the home crowd and cementing their place in football history.

Interruption and Resumption - World War II

The outbreak of World War II disrupted international sports, including the World Cup. The tournament came to a halt, leaving football fans around the world longing for its return. It wasn't until 1950 that the World Cup was revived, with Brazil hosting the event.

The Miracle of Bern - 1954

The 1954 World Cup in Switzerland witnessed one of the greatest upsets in football history. West Germany, a team decimated by World War II, defeated the heavily favored Hungary in a match that became known as the "Miracle of Bern." The tournament showcased football's ability to unite nations and provide hope and healing in the aftermath of war.

Pele and the Brazilian Magic - 1958

The emergence of a young Brazilian prodigy named Pelé marked the 1958 World Cup in Sweden. Pelé's mesmerizing skills and goal-scoring prowess helped Brazil claim their first World Cup title. This victory marked the beginning of Brazil's footballing dynasty and solidified the nation's reputation as the "Soccer Country."

The Iconic 1970 World Cup - Mexico

The 1970 World Cup in Mexico is remembered for its iconic moments, including the "Game of the Century" between Italy and West Germany, which lasted 120 minutes and saw Italy triumph 4-3 after extra time. The tournament also featured a memorable final between Brazil and Italy, with Brazil emerging victorious and securing their third World Cup title.

Maradona's Magic - 1986

The 1986 World Cup in Mexico witnessed the brilliance of Diego Maradona. His "Hand of God" and "Goal of the Century" against England in the quarterfinals showcased his extraordinary talent. Argentina's victory in the tournament established Maradona as one of football's all-time greats.

The Modern Era - Global Spectacle

As we entered the 21st century, the World Cup had become a global spectacle, with billions of viewers tuning in from every corner of the planet. The tournament had expanded to include 32 teams, with nations from Africa, Asia, and Oceania competing alongside the traditional football powerhouses.

The World Cup's ability to bring people together, transcend political differences, and foster cultural exchange has made it a symbol of unity in a divided world. The tournament has also played a significant role in promoting gender equality, with the FIFA Women's World Cup gaining popularity and recognition.

Chapter 9: Football in Times of War and Peace - Historical Context

In the annals of football's history, the sport has not only provided moments of joy and celebration but has also played a significant role during times of conflict and peace. This chapter explores the multifaceted relationship between football and the historical context of war and peace, highlighting how the beautiful game has served as a symbol of resilience, unity, and diplomacy.

The Christmas Truce of 1914 - A Moment of Humanity

Amid the horrors of World War I, a remarkable event occurred on the Western Front in December 1914. Soldiers from opposing sides laid down their weapons and came together to celebrate Christmas. Footballs appeared on the battlefield, and impromptu matches broke out in no-man's land. This remarkable truce, though brief and localized, demonstrated football's power to foster a sense of common humanity even in the darkest of times.

Football as a Form of Resilience

During times of war, football often provided a brief respite from the harsh realities of conflict. Soldiers on the frontlines would organize makeshift matches using whatever they could find as a ball. These games offered moments of camaraderie and escape from the brutality of warfare.

The Miracle of Berne - 1954 World Cup

In the aftermath of World War II, West Germany's victory in the 1954 World Cup, known as the "Miracle of Berne," held profound significance. The tournament symbolized West Germany's post-war resurgence and was a source of pride and hope for the nation. Football, in this context, became a symbol of rebirth and recovery.

The Ivory Coast's Road to Reconciliation - 2006 World Cup

In more recent times, football has played a role in reconciliation efforts in war-torn nations. The Ivory Coast, a country ravaged by civil conflict, found solace and unity in its national football team, the Elephants. The team's qualification for the 2006 World Cup was celebrated as a unifying achievement, and their success on the world stage served as a source of national pride and healing.

Football as Diplomacy - The "Ping Pong Diplomacy" of the 1970s

Football has also been used as a diplomatic tool to bridge political divides. In the 1970s, a series of football matches between the United States and China, known as "Ping Pong Diplomacy," helped thaw relations between the two nations. Football's ability to transcend politics and foster connections between people has been harnessed in various diplomatic efforts.

Chapter 10: Birth of the First Leagues - The English Football League

The late 19th century marked a transformative period in the history of football. In this chapter, we delve into the birth of the first football league in the world, the English Football League (EFL). This pioneering institution laid the foundation for organized football competitions, forever altering the landscape of the beautiful game.

Challenges of Early Football

As football clubs multiplied across England, the need for structured competition became evident. Friendly matches and regional cup competitions were popular, but they lacked the regularity and comprehensive nature of a league system. The diverse rulesets that clubs adhered to further complicated matters.

The Birth of the Football League

In 1888, the Football League was established, forever changing the landscape of football. William McGregor, a director of Aston Villa Football Club, is credited with proposing the idea of a league system to provide consistent and competitive fixtures.

The inaugural season of the Football League featured 12 clubs from the North and Midlands regions of England. The clubs included Aston Villa, Blackburn Rovers, Bolton Wanderers, Burnley, Derby County, Everton, Notts County, Preston North End, Stoke, West Bromwich Albion, Wolverhampton Wanderers, and Accrington.

Preston North End's Invincibles - 1888-89 Season

The first season of the Football League witnessed an astonishing feat by Preston North End, a team that went undefeated throughout the campaign. Their remarkable performance earned them the nickname "The Invincibles." They secured the league title and the FA Cup, cementing their place in football history.

Expanding Horizons - The Second Division

The success of the Football League prompted further expansion. In 1892, the Second Division was introduced, accommodating an additional 12 clubs. This expansion not only allowed for more teams to participate but also introduced the concept of promotion and relegation, where the top and bottom teams of the First Division and Second Division would switch places at the end of each season.

The Football League's Enduring Legacy

The Football League's pioneering model soon became the blueprint for organized football competitions around the world. Other countries followed suit, establishing their own leagues and contributing to the global growth of the sport.

The league system brought structure, consistency, and competitiveness to football, attracting larger audiences and solidifying the sport's popularity. Clubs now had a regular schedule of matches, fostering intense rivalries, and engaging fan bases.

The birth of the English Football League was a seminal moment in the history of football. It introduced the concept of league competition, shaped the way football is organized and played, and laid the foundation for the modern football landscape.

Chapter 11: The Champions League Era - Club Competitions and Rivalries

The dawn of the UEFA Champions League marked a new era in club football, elevating the sport to unprecedented heights of glamour and prestige. In this chapter, we delve into the history of club competitions, the birth of the Champions League, and the fierce rivalries that have defined this era of football.

From Domestic Dominance to European Aspirations

For much of football's early history, clubs focused primarily on domestic competitions. National leagues and cup competitions were the pinnacle of club success. However, as the sport's popularity grew, so did the desire to compete on a broader stage.

The Birth of the European Cup

In 1955, the European Cup was established, marking the beginning of European club competitions. The tournament featured the champions of each European nation's top league, competing in a knockout format. Real Madrid, with legendary players like Alfredo Di Stéfano and Ferenc Puskás, dominated the early years of the competition, winning five consecutive titles from 1956 to 1960.

The Evolution of the Champions League

In 1992, the European Cup was rebranded as the UEFA Champions League, ushering in a new era of club football. The Champions League format expanded to include group stages, providing more opportunities for top clubs to compete. This change also ensured a more extensive array of high-stakes matches, captivating fans and sponsors alike.

The Magnificent Milan - Late 1980s and Early 1990s

AC Milan's dominance in the late 1980s and early 1990s left an indelible mark on the Champions League. With a squad boasting the likes of Marco van Basten, Ruud Gullit, and Paolo Maldini, the Italian giants secured consecutive titles in 1989 and 1990. Milan's tactical prowess and defensive solidity set a standard for the tournament.

The Rivalry: Barcelona vs. Real Madrid

The Champions League era has been defined by fierce club rivalries, none more significant than the El Clásico clash between Barcelona and Real Madrid. Matches between these Spanish giants are not only battles for supremacy but also showcases of footballing excellence. The rivalry has featured iconic players such as Lionel Messi and Cristiano Ronaldo, adding to the drama and intensity.

The English Renaissance

English clubs, led by Manchester United, Liverpool, and Chelsea, have enjoyed a resurgence in the Champions League era. Manchester United's treble-winning season in 1999 and Liverpool's remarkable comeback in the 2005 final are etched in footballing lore. English dominance in the competition has created intense rivalries among Premier League clubs, with Manchester City and Arsenal also vying for European glory.

Chapter 12: International Tournaments - Beyond the World Cup

While the FIFA World Cup stands as the pinnacle of international football, the world of international tournaments extends far beyond this prestigious event. In this chapter, we explore the rich tapestry of international competitions that have captivated football fans around the globe.

The UEFA European Championship - A Continental Showcase

The UEFA European Championship, commonly known as the Euros, is one of the most celebrated international tournaments in the world. First held in 1960, it brings together the top European national teams to compete for glory. The Euros have provided some of football's most iconic moments and have featured legendary players such as Michel Platini, Marco van Basten, and Cristiano Ronaldo.

The Copa America - South America's Finest

The Copa America is the oldest international football tournament, dating back to 1916. It features the national teams of South America and has showcased the incredible talent of players like Pelé, Diego Maradona, and Lionel Messi. The Copa America has a rich history of fierce rivalries and intense competition, making it a highlight of the international football calendar.

Africa Cup of Nations - A Continent United by Football

The Africa Cup of Nations (AFCON) has played a significant role in fostering football's growth on the African continent. Established in 1957, it has been a platform for African nations to showcase their footballing talent. The tournament has witnessed the rise of African football stars, including George Weah, Samuel Eto'o, and Didier Drogba.

The Asian Cup - Football in the East

The AFC Asian Cup has become a showcase for Asian footballing prowess since its inception in 1956. Nations like Japan, South Korea, and Saudi Arabia have risen to prominence on the international stage through their performances in the tournament. The Asian Cup has also helped bridge cultural divides, promoting unity and cooperation across the continent.

The Impact of International Tournaments

International tournaments serve as a celebration of football's global appeal and the cultural diversity of the sport. These competitions not only provide thrilling matches but also offer a platform for nations to showcase their identity and pride on the world stage. The passion of fans, the drama of knockout rounds, and the quest for international glory make these tournaments a cherished part of football's heritage.

Chapter 13: Football and Society - Politics, Economics, and Identity

Football is not merely a game played on a pitch; it is a reflection of society itself, intertwined with politics, economics, and identity. In this chapter, we delve into the complex and multifaceted relationship between football and the broader societal forces that shape the beautiful game.

Football and Politics - A Mirror of the World

Throughout its history, football has mirrored the political climate of the times. From the rise of fascist regimes in the 1930s using football as a propaganda tool to the boycotts and protests during the apartheid era in South Africa, the sport has been both a reflection and a battleground for political ideologies.

The Tragedy of Heysel and Hillsborough

The tragedies of the Heysel Stadium disaster in 1985 and the Hillsborough Stadium disaster in 1989 serve as stark reminders of the intertwined relationship between football and politics. These events had far-reaching consequences, leading to changes in stadium safety regulations and policing.

Football and Economics - The Business of the Game

Football has evolved into a massive global industry, with billions of dollars flowing through the sport each year. From lucrative broadcasting deals to commercial sponsorships and merchandise sales, the economic impact of football is undeniable. Clubs like Manchester United, Real

Madrid, and Barcelona are not only football powerhouses but also major economic entities.

However, this commercialization of the sport has also raised questions about financial inequality, the role of mega-rich owners, and the commodification of players. The tension between the economic interests of clubs and the passion of fans has become a central theme in modern football.

Football and Identity - The Heart of Communities

Football is deeply intertwined with the identity of communities, nations, and regions. The support for a local club or national team often transcends mere fandom; it becomes an integral part of an individual's sense of self. The chants, traditions, and rituals of football fans reflect their cultural identities and affiliations.

Women's Football - Breaking Barriers

The growth of women's football has been a significant development in recent years. As women's teams gain recognition and support, the sport is challenging traditional gender norms and breaking down barriers. The success of tournaments like the FIFA Women's World Cup has been a testament to the global appeal of women's football.

Chapter 14: Football and the Media - The Impact of Television and the Internet

The evolution of football has been significantly influenced by the media, transforming the sport from local pastime to global spectacle. In this chapter, we explore the profound impact of television and the internet on football, and how these mediums have shaped the way we experience the beautiful game.

Television's Arrival - Football for the Masses

The advent of television in the mid-20th century brought football into the living rooms of millions. The 1966 FIFA World Cup in England marked a turning point as it became the first World Cup to be televised worldwide. This expansion of the audience not only elevated the sport's popularity but also changed the dynamics of how it was consumed.

The Globalization of Football

Television broadcasts allowed fans to follow their favorite teams and players from across the globe. Icons like Pelé, Johan Cruyff, and Diego Maradona became international sensations, captivating audiences far beyond their home countries. International club competitions like the European Cup (now UEFA Champions League) and the Copa Libertadores reached global audiences, further fueling the globalization of football.

Television and the Financial Boom

Television rights became a major source of revenue for clubs and governing bodies. The massive sums offered by broadcasters allowed clubs to invest in top talent and state-of-the-art stadiums, escalating the level of competition and raising the sport's profile.

The Internet Revolution - Access Anytime, Anywhere

The internet revolutionized football consumption by providing fans with instant access to news, highlights, and matches from around the world. Websites, forums, and social media platforms allowed fans to connect, discuss, and share their passion for the sport.

The Rise of Online Streaming

The proliferation of online streaming services has further democratized football consumption. Fans can now watch matches and events from leagues and countries they may not have had access to in the past. Streaming has also allowed smaller clubs and leagues to gain international recognition.

The Impact on Fan Engagement

The internet and social media have reshaped how fans engage with the sport. Platforms like Twitter, Facebook, and Instagram have become integral to the fan experience, enabling fans to interact with players, clubs, and fellow supporters. These platforms have also been used for fan-driven initiatives, such as crowdfunding campaigns and protests against club ownership.

Chapter 15: The Beautiful Game on the Big Screen - Movies and Documentaries

Football's allure extends beyond the confines of the pitch, captivating audiences on the big screen through movies and documentaries. In this chapter, we explore the world of football in cinema, examining how these films have celebrated the sport, its legends, and its impact on society.

"Escape to Victory" (1981) - The Beautiful Game in a Prison Camp

"Escape to Victory," directed by John Huston, is a unique blend of war drama and football. Set during World War II, the film tells the story of Allied prisoners of war who form a football team to face their Nazi captors on the pitch. Starring football icon Pelé and Hollywood legend Michael Caine, the film captures the resilience and camaraderie that football can inspire even in the direst circumstances.

"Bend It Like Beckham" (2002) - Breaking Stereotypes

"Gurinder Chadha's "Bend It Like Beckham" explores the challenges faced by a young British-Indian girl who aspires to play football against her traditional family's wishes. The film showcases the power of football to challenge gender stereotypes and cultural norms, resonating with audiences worldwide.

"The Damned United" (2009) - The Brian Clough Story

"The Damned United" delves into the life and career of legendary football manager Brian Clough. Directed by Tom Hooper and starring

Michael Sheen as Clough, the film chronicles Clough's tumultuous 44-day tenure as the manager of Leeds United. It offers a glimpse into the complex personality of one of football's most iconic figures.

Football Documentaries - Capturing the Essence of the Sport

Football documentaries have also left an indelible mark on the world of cinema. Films like "Senna" (2010), which chronicles the life of Formula 1 legend Ayrton Senna, and "Maradona" (2019), which explores the tumultuous career of Diego Maradona, have provided intimate portraits of sporting greatness and human complexity.

The Impact of Football Cinema

Football movies and documentaries have the power to inspire, challenge, and entertain. They celebrate the sport's universal appeal, its ability to break down barriers, and its capacity to transcend the boundaries of culture and nationality. These films have allowed fans and non-fans alike to connect with the heart and soul of the beautiful game.

Chapter 16: The Evolution of Football Stadiums

The evolution of football stadiums is a testament to the ever-changing landscape of the sport. In this chapter, we explore the architectural, technological, and cultural developments that have shaped the modern football stadium, transforming it into a hub of excitement, passion, and entertainment.

The Birth of Football Stadiums

In the early days of football, matches were played on open fields or local parks, with minimal spectator facilities. As the sport's popularity grew, the need for dedicated stadiums became apparent. The first football-specific stadium, Bramall Lane in Sheffield, England, was opened in 1855.

The Era of Terraces and Stands

The 20th century saw the construction of iconic terraced stands, such as the famous "Kop" at Anfield and the "Stretford End" at Old Trafford. These terraces accommodated large crowds and created an electric atmosphere on match days. However, safety concerns and tragedies, such as the Hillsborough disaster, led to changes in stadium design and regulations.

The Rise of All-Seater Stadiums

The 1990 Taylor Report, commissioned in the aftermath of the Hillsborough disaster, recommended that top-tier stadiums in England become all-seater venues to enhance safety and comfort. This ushered in a new era of stadium design, with the removal of terraces and the introduction of individual seats.

The Modern Football Arena

Modern football stadiums are architectural marvels, designed not only for safety and comfort but also to enhance the fan experience. Features like VIP suites, corporate boxes, and fan zones cater to diverse audiences. Technological advancements, including giant video screens and high-speed Wi-Fi, allow fans to stay connected during matches.

The Environmental Impact

In recent years, sustainability and environmental concerns have played a significant role in stadium design. Many new stadiums are constructed with eco-friendly materials, energy-efficient lighting, and renewable energy sources. Green initiatives are becoming an integral part of the football stadium landscape.

Iconic Stadiums of the 21st Century

Stadiums like Wembley in London, the Allianz Arena in Munich, and the Camp Nou in Barcelona have become iconic symbols of football culture. Their unique designs, capacity, and history make them must-visit destinations for fans around the world.

Chapter 17: The Roar of the Crowd - Football Fan Culture

<hr>

ootball fan culture is a vibrant and integral aspect of the sport, contributing to its unique atmosphere and global appeal. In this chapter, we delve into the passionate world of football fandom, exploring the rituals, chants, and traditions that define the beautiful game's fan experience.

The Heart and Soul of Football

Football fans are the heartbeat of the sport, infusing stadiums with energy and creating an unforgettable atmosphere. Their unwavering support, colorful banners, and deafening chants make football matches a spectacle unlike any other.

Matchday Rituals

Matchday rituals are an essential part of football fan culture. Supporters gather before games in pubs, bars, and fan zones to share pre-match excitement. Traditional foods, drinks, and songs create a sense of unity and anticipation.

Chants and Songs

Football fans are renowned for their creative chants and songs. These anthems, often rooted in local culture and history, unite supporters and inspire players. From Liverpool's "You'll Never Walk Alone" to Borussia Dortmund's "Yellow Wall" chants, these melodies are etched in football lore.

Rivalries and Derbies

Football rivalries add drama and intensity to the sport. Matches between rival teams are often the most anticipated and emotionally charged. The North West Derby between Liverpool and Everton or the El Clásico clash between Barcelona and Real Madrid are prime examples of football rivalries that transcend the sport.

Tifos and Banners

Elaborate tifos and banners are a visual spectacle in football stadiums. These displays are meticulously crafted and often carry powerful messages or celebrate club history. They add color and grandeur to the fan experience.

Away Supporters

Away supporters are the embodiment of dedication, traveling great distances to support their team. They bring their unique chants and passion to opposing stadiums, creating a lively atmosphere that adds to the spectacle of the game.

Football Hooliganism

While most football fans are passionate and well-behaved, hooliganism has been a dark underbelly of fan culture. Acts of violence and disorderly conduct by a minority of fans have marred the sport's image and led to strict security measures at stadiums.

The Global Impact of Fan Culture

Football fan culture has transcended borders, with supporters' clubs and fan groups established around the world. Social media has allowed fans to connect and share their passion, breaking down geographical barriers and fostering a sense of global community.

Chapter 18: Iconic Moments - Memorable Matches and Goals

Football is a sport filled with moments that etch themselves into the annals of history. In this chapter, we relive the drama, excitement, and brilliance of some of the most iconic moments in the beautiful game, from unforgettable matches to legendary goals.

The "Hand of God" and the "Goal of the Century" - Diego Maradona (1986 World Cup)

Diego Maradona's performance in the 1986 World Cup in Mexico remains the stuff of legend. In a quarter-final match against England, Maradona scored what would become two of the most famous goals in football history. His controversial "Hand of God" goal, followed by a mesmerizing dribble past five England defenders, known as the "Goal of the Century," showcased Maradona's genius.

The Miracle of Istanbul - Liverpool vs. AC Milan (2005 UEFA Champions League Final)

The 2005 UEFA Champions League Final between Liverpool and AC Milan is considered one of the greatest comebacks in football history. Liverpool, trailing 3-0 at halftime, staged a miraculous recovery to level the score at 3-3 and eventually win the match in a penalty shootout. It was a night of unforgettable drama at Istanbul's Atatürk Olympic Stadium.

The "Invincibles" - Arsenal's Unbeaten League Season (2003-04)

Arsenal's 2003-04 Premier League season stands as a remarkable achievement. Coached by Arsène Wenger, the team went unbeaten throughout the league campaign, earning them the nickname "The Invincibles." Their feat of 26 wins and 12 draws remains unmatched in the modern era of English football.

The Hand of God Reversed - Diego Maradona (2020)

In a symbolic moment, Diego Maradona recreated his famous "Hand of God" goal during an exhibition match in 2020. This time, it was a playful tribute to his own iconic moment, showcasing the enduring impact of football history.

The "Rumble in the Jungle" - Zaire vs. Brazil (1974 World Cup)

In one of the most bizarre moments in World Cup history, Zaire's Mwepu Ilunga sprinted out of the defensive wall and kicked the ball away before Brazil could take a free-kick. The moment captured the unpredictability and audacity that football can produce on the grandest stage.

Chapter 19: Modern Game Tactics and Strategies

The evolution of football is not limited to its history; it extends to the ever-changing tactics and strategies that define the modern game. In this chapter, we delve into the tactical innovations, playing styles, and strategies that have shaped contemporary football.

Total Football - The Dutch Revolution

In the 1970s, Dutch football introduced the concept of "Total Football," which emphasized fluidity, versatility, and the ability of outfield players to interchange positions seamlessly. Under the guidance of Rinus Michels and Johan Cruyff, the Dutch national team showcased this style in the 1974 FIFA World Cup, leaving a lasting impact on the sport.

Tiki-Taka - Spain's Midfield Mastery

Spain's tiki-taka style of play, characterized by short passes, quick ball circulation, and possession dominance, became a hallmark of their success in international football. Under the management of Vicente del Bosque and with players like Xavi Hernandez and Andres Iniesta, Spain won consecutive European Championships in 2008 and 2012, as well as the 2010 FIFA World Cup.

Gegenpressing - Klopp's High-Intensity Game

Jurgen Klopp's "Gegenpressing" philosophy at Borussia Dortmund and later at Liverpool revolutionized pressing and counter-pressing tactics. His teams exhibit high-intensity pressing to regain possession immediately after losing the ball, making them formidable opponents and earning Liverpool the 2018-19 UEFA Champions League title.

Tactical Innovations - Pep Guardiola's Possession-Based Football

Pep Guardiola's managerial philosophy centers around possession-based football, where his teams prioritize ball retention and positional play. His tactical innovations, notably at FC Barcelona and Manchester City, have influenced the way modern teams approach the game.

The Rise of the High Press - Klopp vs. Guardiola

The tactical battles between Jurgen Klopp and Pep Guardiola in the English Premier League have showcased the contrast between high pressing and possession-based football. Their clashes have become defining moments in the league's recent history, captivating fans with their tactical acumen.

The Importance of Data and Analysis

The use of data and analytics has become integral to modern football. Clubs employ sophisticated tracking and analysis tools to gain insights into player performance, opposition strategies, and match preparation. Data-driven decision-making has transformed player recruitment and team tactics.

Chapter 20: Challenges and Controversies - From Corruption to Diversity

———

The world of football, like any other, has faced its share of challenges and controversies. In this chapter, we examine some of the most pressing issues that have arisen in the sport, from corruption scandals to the ongoing quest for diversity and inclusion.

Match-Fixing and Corruption

One of the most significant challenges football has faced is match-fixing and corruption. Scandals have rocked the sport at various levels, from domestic leagues to international competitions. The infiltration of criminal elements seeking financial gain has tarnished the integrity of the game.

FIFA Corruption Scandal (2015)

The FIFA corruption scandal of 2015 brought to light widespread corruption and bribery within the world governing body of football. High-ranking FIFA officials were implicated in a bribery and kickback scheme related to the awarding of World Cup hosting rights. The scandal led to the ousting of several officials and prompted reforms within FIFA.

Racism and Discrimination

Racism and discrimination have plagued football, both on and off the pitch. Players and fans have been subjected to racial abuse, highlighting the need for concerted efforts to combat bigotry and promote diversity. Organizations like Kick It Out and initiatives like "No Room for Racism" aim to eradicate discrimination from the sport.

Gender Inequality

Women's football has made significant strides, but gender inequality remains a challenge. Disparities in pay, opportunities, and resources between men's and women's football continue to be a point of contention. The fight for equal pay and recognition for female players is ongoing.

Homophobia and LGBTQ+ Representation

Homophobia has been a concern in football, with LGBTQ+ players and fans often facing discrimination. Organizations like Stonewall and initiatives like "Football v Homophobia" aim to create a more inclusive environment for LGBTQ+ individuals in the sport.

Financial Disparities

Financial disparities between top-tier and lower-tier clubs have widened, raising concerns about competitive balance. Superclubs with vast resources dominate domestic and international competitions, while smaller clubs struggle to compete. Efforts to address financial fair play and revenue distribution are ongoing.

Chapter 21: Future of Football - Technology and Innovation

The future of football is a horizon filled with exciting possibilities driven by technology and innovation. In this chapter, we explore the ways in which advancements in science and technology are shaping the future of the beautiful game.

VAR (Video Assistant Referee) - A Game Changer

VAR has had a significant impact on the sport, introducing a new layer of precision and fairness to refereeing decisions. While it has generated debate and controversy, VAR's potential to minimize errors and enhance the accuracy of match officiating is undeniable.

Goal-Line Technology - Decisive Moments

Goal-line technology has settled debates about whether the ball crossed the goal line, providing instant and conclusive decisions. It has been instrumental in ensuring that goals are awarded fairly.

Player Tracking and Analytics

The use of GPS trackers and wearable technology has allowed teams to monitor player performance more comprehensively. Data analytics provide insights into players' physical and tactical capabilities, helping coaches make informed decisions.

Biomechanics and Injury Prevention

Advancements in biomechanics have contributed to injury prevention and rehabilitation. Understanding players' movement patterns and physical stress allows for personalized training programs and injury management.

Fan Engagement and Virtual Experiences

Virtual reality (VR) and augmented reality (AR) technologies are revolutionizing fan engagement. VR allows fans to experience matches in immersive virtual environments, while AR enhances the in-stadium experience with additional information and interactive elements.

Sustainability and Eco-Friendly Initiatives

Football is increasingly embracing sustainability and eco-friendly initiatives. Stadiums are being designed with energy-efficient features, and clubs are reducing their carbon footprint. Initiatives like "green" kits made from recycled materials are becoming more common.

E-Sports and Digital Competitions

E-sports, such as FIFA video game tournaments, have gained popularity and recognition in the football world. They provide a new platform for competition and engage a younger generation of fans.

Chapter 22: Football's Greatest Players - Profiles and Achievements

———

Football's history is adorned with legendary players who have left an indelible mark on the sport. In this chapter, we pay tribute to some of the greatest footballers to ever grace the pitch, highlighting their remarkable careers and achievements.

Pelé - The King of Football

Pelé, the Brazilian icon, is often regarded as the greatest footballer of all time. He won three FIFA World Cups (1958, 1962, and 1970), scored over 1,000 career goals, and dazzled the world with his skill, vision, and goal-scoring prowess.

Diego Maradona - The Hand of God

Diego Maradona, the Argentine maestro, is celebrated for his mesmerizing dribbling and creativity. He led Argentina to victory in the 1986 World Cup and is remembered for his "Hand of God" and "Goal of the Century" in a quarter-final match against England.

Johan Cruyff - Total Football Pioneer

Johan Cruyff, the Dutch visionary, introduced the concept of "Total Football" and was a key figure in the rise of FC Barcelona's football philosophy. His influence as a player and manager revolutionized the sport.

Lionel Messi - The Modern Magician

Lionel Messi, often compared to Pelé and Maradona, has amassed numerous individual awards, including multiple Ballon d'Or titles. His dribbling, vision, and goal-scoring prowess have made him one of the most celebrated players of his generation.

Cristiano Ronaldo - The Goal Machine

Cristiano Ronaldo, the Portuguese superstar, is known for his incredible athleticism and goal-scoring ability. He has won multiple Ballon d'Or awards and has been a dominant force in both domestic and international football.

Michel Platini - The French Maestro

Michel Platini, the French midfield maestro, was a three-time Ballon d'Or winner. He led the French national team to victory in the 1984 UEFA European Championship and had a distinguished club career with AS Saint-Étienne and Juventus.

Brazil's Samba Stars - Garrincha and Zico

Garrincha, the Brazilian dribbling wizard, and Zico, the creative genius, left an indelible mark on Brazilian football. Garrincha won two World Cups (1958 and 1962), while Zico was renowned for his skill and leadership.

Chapter 23: Influential Coaches and Managers

Behind every successful football team stands a visionary coach or manager. In this chapter, we explore the influential figures who have shaped the tactics, philosophy, and success of football clubs and national teams around the world.

Sir Matt Busby - The Father of Manchester United

Sir Matt Busby, the legendary manager of Manchester United, is revered for his role in rebuilding the club after the Munich air disaster in 1958. Under his leadership, Manchester United achieved unprecedented success, including winning the European Cup in 1968.

Sir Alex Ferguson - The Master of Longevity

Sir Alex Ferguson's tenure at Manchester United from 1986 to 2013 is marked by his incredible longevity and success. He won numerous Premier League titles and two UEFA Champions League titles, establishing Manchester United as a global powerhouse.

Arrigo Sacchi - The Architect of Italian Football

Arrigo Sacchi, the Italian coach, is known for his revolutionary defensive tactics and pressing game. He led AC Milan to back-to-back European Cup victories in 1989 and 1990 and left a lasting impact on football philosophy.

Pep Guardiola - The Tiki-Taka Tactician

Pep Guardiola's innovative approach to possession-based football and tactical flexibility has earned him acclaim. He has managed successful teams at FC Barcelona, Bayern Munich, and Manchester City, winning numerous league titles and Champions League trophies.

Jurgen Klopp - The Gegenpressing Guru

Jurgen Klopp's high-intensity pressing style, known as Gegenpressing, has transformed clubs like Borussia Dortmund and Liverpool. He led Liverpool to the 2018-19 UEFA Champions League title and ended the club's long Premier League title drought in 2020.

Vicente del Bosque - Spain's Silent Success

Vicente del Bosque masterminded Spain's golden era, winning the 2010 FIFA World Cup and the 2012 UEFA European Championship. His calm and collected demeanor guided Spain to unprecedented international success.

Arsene Wenger - The Professor of Football

Arsene Wenger's tenure at Arsenal brought a new era of football to English shores. His emphasis on nutrition, tactics, and attractive football revolutionized the Premier League.

Chapter 24: The Enduring Legacy of Football

Football's legacy extends far beyond the confines of the pitch. In this final chapter, we reflect on the enduring impact of the beautiful game on society, culture, and the lives of millions around the world.

Football as a Unifying Force

Football has the unique ability to bring people together across cultures, languages, and borders. It fosters a sense of belonging and unity, creating a global community of fans who share a common love for the sport.

Football and Identity

Football often plays a significant role in shaping individual and collective identities. It can be a source of pride, a reflection of local culture, and a symbol of national identity. The colors of a football club's jersey or the songs sung by fans can carry deep emotional significance.

Football and Social Change

Football has been a catalyst for social change and progress. It has been used to raise awareness about important issues, promote inclusivity, and inspire positive actions. Initiatives like "Football for All" and "Football Beyond Borders" harness the sport's power for social impact.

Football as Entertainment

Football is not just a sport; it's a form of entertainment that captivates billions of viewers around the world. The drama, excitement, and unpredictability of matches make football a global spectacle.

Football's Contribution to Health and Fitness

The sport encourages physical activity and fitness, promoting a healthier lifestyle for millions. Grassroots programs and community football initiatives encourage participation and well-being.

The Economic Impact of Football

Football is a significant driver of the global economy. It generates revenue through broadcasting rights, sponsorship deals, and merchandise sales. It also creates jobs and spurs economic development, especially in regions with strong football traditions.

Football's Educational Value

Football can instill valuable life skills such as teamwork, discipline, and perseverance. Youth academies and coaching programs teach young players not only about the game but also about important life lessons.

The Joy of the Game

At its core, football is about joy and passion. It's about the joy of scoring a goal, the thrill of a last-minute winner, and the camaraderie of supporting a team. It brings happiness to countless lives.

The enduring legacy of football is a testament to its universal appeal and cultural significance. It transcends boundaries, enriches lives, and inspires generations. As we conclude our exploration of football's history, we celebrate the captivating stories, legendary players, influential coaches, and the countless individuals who have contributed to making the beautiful game a global phenomenon.

Chapter 25: Reflections on Football's Unforgettable Journey

As we reach the final chapter of our journey through the history and impact of football, it's time to reflect on the beautiful game's enduring and remarkable journey.

A Unifying Force

Football has an extraordinary power to unite people from all walks of life, transcending boundaries of race, nationality, and religion. It is a language understood by millions, fostering a sense of togetherness that is unrivaled in the world of sports.

A Source of Inspiration

The stories of legendary players, visionary coaches, and passionate fans are a testament to the sport's ability to inspire. Football teaches us about determination, teamwork, and the pursuit of excellence. It shows us that dreams can be realized through dedication and hard work.

A Catalyst for Change

Football has the potential to drive positive change in society. It has been a platform for addressing important issues such as racism, discrimination, and social inequality. The sport's influence extends beyond the pitch, encouraging us to stand up for what is right and just.

A Global Phenomenon

From local pitches to grand stadiums, from grassroots initiatives to international tournaments, football's reach is vast and all-encompassing.

It is a spectacle that captivates billions, a source of joy and passion that unites fans across the world.

A Timeless Legacy

Football's legacy is timeless. It is a legacy of iconic moments, legendary players, and unforgettable matches. It is a legacy of dreams fulfilled and aspirations kindled. It is a legacy that will continue to shape the world for generations to come.

Conclusion

As we close the final chapter of our exploration, we celebrate the enduring and remarkable journey of football. It is a journey filled with triumphs and challenges, passion and inspiration, and moments that will live on in the hearts of fans forever.

Football is more than a sport; it is a way of life, a source of joy, and a symbol of unity. It is a story that continues to be written by players, coaches, and fans alike. It is a story that we all contribute to, in our own unique ways, as we embrace the beautiful game and its boundless capacity to bring people together.

In the realm of sports, few endeavors rival the global phenomenon that is football. From its humble beginnings on muddy fields to the grandeur of modern stadiums, football's journey through time has been nothing short of extraordinary. As we conclude our exploration, we are left with an abiding appreciation for the enduring legacy and profound impact of the beautiful game.

Football is more than a sport; it is a cultural touchstone that unites people across the world. It is a universal language, spoken by millions, transcending barriers of language, nationality, and creed. It is a source of joy, passion, and inspiration, igniting the hearts and minds of fans young and old.

The pages of football's history are filled with iconic moments, legendary players, visionary coaches, and passionate fans. From the wizardry of Pelé to the artistry of Messi, from the tactical brilliance of Cruyff to the managerial acumen of Ferguson, from the electric atmospheres of Anfield to the passionate support of the Maracanã, football's tapestry is woven with stories that resonate in the hearts of fans around the world.

But football is not just about what happens on the pitch; it is also about the values it instills. It teaches us about teamwork, perseverance, and the pursuit of excellence. It shows us that dreams can be realized through dedication and hard work. It inspires us to stand up for justice, equality, and the betterment of society.

As we reflect on football's journey, we celebrate its ability to endure and evolve. It has weathered challenges, controversies, and changes, emerging stronger and more vibrant than ever. It continues to capture the imagination of billions, creating moments of shared joy and unity that are etched in our collective memory.

The beautiful game's legacy is timeless, and its future is filled with promise. It is a journey that will continue to be written by players, coaches, and fans alike. It is a journey that transcends time, leaving an indelible mark on the world.

In closing, we honor the enduring legacy of football and the countless individuals who have contributed to its rich history. Football's beauty lies not just in its goals, but in the stories it tells, the dreams it inspires, and the unity it fosters. As we bid farewell to this exploration, we do so with gratitude for the privilege of celebrating the beautiful game and the remarkable journey it has taken us on.

The beautiful game endures, and so does our love for it. Thank you for joining us on this unforgettable journey.

Don't miss out!

Visit the website below and you can sign up to receive emails whenever PA BOOKS publishes a new book. There's no charge and no obligation.

https://books2read.com/r/B-A-STTAB-RNZOC

BOOKS 2 READ

Connecting independent readers to independent writers.